# Cuddle Meditation:

## *How to Build Self-Soothing Skills with Snuggles*

By Kristene Geering

Edited by Lisa D. Thompson

*This publication is designed to give readers general information and strategies, but should not be used as a diagnostic tool or substitute for professional support. Neither the publisher nor the author should be construed as offering individualized advice or services. If you need further support, please seek out a licensed, certified or credentialed professional as appropriate.*

Published by Let Us Learn Together

*To my husband, who taught me that healthy, loving relationships truly heal.*

# Table of Contents

Introduction ................................................. 1

    How Brains & Bodies Work Together ......... 3

    Adapt & Adjust As Your Child Grows ........ 12

    Tuning In to Your Kid & Their Cues ........... 14

The Tools ................................................. 19

    Bell Bowl Meditation ................................. 22

    Quiet vs Loud ........................................ 24

    Breathing Buddies ................................... 27

    Snorkel Breathing ................................... 29

    Breath Ball ........................................... 31

    Big, Burly Bubble Breaths ......................... 33

    Magic Wands ......................................... 35

    Hot Cocoa Magic .................................... 37

    Peace in a Jar ........................................ 39

    Cuddle Meditation .................................. 42

    Feelings Collage ..................................... 44

    Oooo...or, "Blech?" ................................. 46

    Dinosaur Feet ....................................... 48

    Cloud Dough ........................................ 50

    Silent Helpers ....................................... 52

    Rainbow Bubble Painting ......................... 54

    Special Stones ....................................... 56

    Thankful Hands ..................................... 58

    Swing & Sing ........................................ 60

    Spin & Grin .......................................... 62

Conclusion ............................................... 64

# Introduction

Being a parent is one of the most rewarding, challenging, joyful, stressful, exasperating and every-other-emotion events that can happen to a person. It's a roller coaster, for sure. You can go from smiling ear-to-ear to screaming bloody murder in the amount of time it takes to say, "We're out of chicken nuggets."

And while there are many ways to become a parent, once it happens, we all get knocked upside the head with this: the sudden overwhelming and deeply humbling experience of realizing that we are now responsible for the health and well-being of a small human. Until death do us part. Without an instruction manual.

Parenting is not for the faint of heart, am I right?

That's where this workbook comes in. When you're done with it, you'll feel more comfortable in your parenting your small human because you will:

- Have a general understanding of how their brains and bodies work together
- Know how to adjust and adapt as your child grows
- Know how to tune in to your specific kid and their cues
- Have a full set of tools you know will work with your child

# How Brains & Bodies Work Together

*Co-Regulation Leads to Self-Regulation*

There are a lot of parenting books out there explaining in detail why children tend to fly off the handle so easily, but let me give it to you in a nutshell: Their brain simply isn't done baking.

The part of the brain that helps regulate emotions is located in the frontal lobe, which isn't done developing until (wait for it . . .) after adolescence. Yeah. It really takes that long. I'll give you a moment.

But as parents, we have a super power when it comes to helping our kids develop this part of their brain. We can't force development to unfold faster, but we *can* create conditions ideal for that development. We can help our kids develop the skills of self-soothing through what I like to call "letting your kid borrow your brain." This happens through the magic of *mirror neurons*.

Our brains are wired to pick up on the behaviors and feelings of the people around us from a very young age because it keeps us safe. If I'm hiking with a group of people, getting lost in nature and enjoying the sights and surroundings, and I notice that a few people ahead of me have just stopped in their tracks and gasped loudly, I don't necessarily need to see the brown bear 100 yards up the trail in order to understand that we might be in danger. Their behavior tells me, "Uh oh! Stop walking and pay attention."

Apply this to parenting. If you're a child, and your mom or dad is feeling relaxed and happy, that signals that it's safe to explore the world and learn stuff. But if mom or dad seems stressed or scared, that signals that something's wrong—that it might be time to hide or run away. Your child is tuned in to you and your moods in a way that nobody else is because their survival literally depends on it.

The good news about this is that your ability to stay calm and grounded when they're freaking out or upset or throwing a tantrum can help bring them back from the Land of Meltdowns. You're a beacon of calm in a storm of chaos and big, scary feelings. And when your child gets lost in that storm, your calm and steady presence is how they'll find their way back.

When you practice this skill (and it takes practice!), you're doing something called **co-regulation**. Regulation, or being able to manage big feelings, isn't something you can learn at any age. Like other developmental skills, you have to grow into it. Just like we wouldn't expect a 2-year-old to make dinner for everyone, we can't expect them to know how to regulate their emotions, because they don't have the brain structures in place. One of the best ways you can help your child build that skill is through co-regulation. You're basically showing their brain how it's done, so over time they'll have that blueprint as they build the connections and structures to start regulating themselves. Remember: **Co-regulation is the basis for self-regulation**.

*The Five—I Mean Eight—Senses*

Another way our bodies and brains work together is seen in the way we take information from our senses so we can understand and move through the world. This can have a profound impact on our ability to manage our emotions, especially when we don't realize what's happening.

Take "hangry," for example. You probably know someone who gets hangry. Could be your kid (very common), could be your partner—or if you're like me, it could be you! In case you haven't seen that Snickers commercial, hangry is when someone suddenly flies off the handle for reasons no one else can understand—but once they eat, they're suddenly a different person.

Why is that? Snickers did not make this up.

It makes sense when you understand that your brain's primary function is to keep you safe. Your senses are constantly on the lookout for any kind of threat. They feed this information to your brain, and your brain's job is to sort through all that info as quickly as possible to make sure you're safe—it does this on a mostly subconscious level.

The lower part of your brain is where your stress response lives. If the brain detects even a hint of a threat, your stress response kicks in. This is often called the fight-or-flight response and involves an increase in certain chemicals, like cortisol and adrenaline, that prepare your body for some kind of immediate action. How does the brain detect threats? Through the information collected by the senses.

Back to hangry. When the brain detects that there's a hunger signal that isn't being addressed, it senses that there's a threat. The longer the hunger builds up, the more your brain is like, "Danger!" So, some folks slip into their stress response until their brain gets the sensory input that hunger is no longer a problem.

But wait, you might think, how is hunger part of the five senses I learned in school? It turns out there are a lot of ways to look at how the brain perceives the world, both around and within the body. You can think of your brain as living inside a box, with no communication with the outside world other than what it receives through your senses. That information is coming in constantly, 24/7, with no stops. If you were consciously aware of every signal that came in that would be uncomfortable to say the least. More than likely, it would put you on the fast track to insanity.

So, our brains and bodies have learned to coordinate and process that information at a level below awareness. After this information is processed, our attention is directed toward what is deemed the highest priority of the moment. Put it all together and that's what we call "sensory processing" or "sensory integration."

One of the most common ways to talk about sensory processing is to refer to eight senses. Why add in an extra three senses? Because you really want to cover all the streams of information your brain is taking in, including things like body position, balance, and what's going on *inside* your body.

Becoming familiar with all eight senses and how your child processes them offers you another parental super power. It gives you the ability to know what's going on with your child, so you can decide in the moment what you want to do to help your kid calm down.

Here are the eight senses that may be behind some of your child's meltdowns:

👁 *Visual* (**Sight**) is at the top of the list most people have when they think about the senses. When a child has difficulty seeing, it can have a profound impact on their overall development and academic performance. While vision challenges can often be addressed with glasses or contacts, sometimes the challenges are a bit more nuanced. Kids who are easily over-stimulated with what they see, for example, may benefit from having a room that has minimal wall art and/or clean, tidy surfaces.

*Auditory* (**Hearing**) is the next sense most people think of, as it's also known to impact a kid's growth and development. If there are challenges with hearing, an audiologist can help detect problems and come up with technological solutions like hearing aids or cochlear implants. But this sense can also overwhelm kids who are sensitive to certain types of noise, like vacuums or hair dryers, or are bothered by volume. Something as simple as turning down or off background music can have an instantly calming effect on some folks.

*Gustatory* (**Taste**) is an important sense for the brain to track when it comes to safety. Flavors such as extreme bitterness are often a sign that something is inedible and should be spat out immediately. As kids begin to explore what foods they do and don't like, any hint of bitterness might be the reason behind a refusal to eat. But young tongues are also very sensitive, so they may have a harder time with strong tastes like sour, as well.

*Olfactory* (**Smell**) is closely linked to safety, like taste. It's also something that can be very hard to put into words. When we encounter a strong, unpleasant smell, our brains tell our bodies to kick it into high gear and get away. Kids with a particularly sensitive sense of smell may not be able to tell you why they're withdrawing from situations.

*Tactile*         (**Touch**) is another sense we easily associate with safety. If you touch something sharp, like the spines of a cactus, your immediate and unconscious response is to recoil and move away from the plant. Kids with a sensitive sense of touch may cause hurt feelings when they recoil away from gentle touches, even though that reaction has nothing to do with the person and everything to do with the touch their body perceives.

*Proprioceptive* (**Body Position**) is our sense of where we feel **pressure**, and therefore our body's position. If you close your eyes, for example, you can tell whether your legs are crossed. This is because your body senses whether there's pressure at your knee, in your foot, etc. Proprioception can be a calming input for many people (think swaddling or massage).

**Ť** *Vestibular* **(Balance)** is how your body is oriented in space. It's how you know if you're upside down or not. Vestibular input can also be calming for some people (think swinging or rocking).

*Interoceptive* **(Internal Sense)** is how you interpret the signals from **inside your body**. This is how you know if you're hungry or thirsty or if you need to go to the bathroom. Interoception is very difficult to learn, as it's such an individual thing and not easily shared with others. Adults often have trouble with some of their interception, mistaking boredom for hunger, for example. *One of the best ways to learn about your own body's interoception is to practice mindfulness.* The act of paying attention to your own experiences helps you more accurately identify what your body is trying to tell you.

*Adapt and Adjust as Your Child Grows*

How does knowing about these senses and how they interact with the brain help your child build self-soothing skills? It helps because you'll learn, over time, if your child is sensitive to loud noises. You may choose, then, to put ear protectors on them before going to an amusement park. Or you know to keep the radio volume under a 6 in the car. You can also help your child learn about this trait in themselves, and teach them how to advocate for their needs. When they're older (and their brains are more developed), you can use everything you've learned to help them come up with coping strategies for the times when things are just loud and outside of your control.

No matter where you are on your parenting journey, you've seen how quickly your growing child changes. Sometimes it can feel like they grew an inch overnight! But growth and development in the brain can be harder to detect, and it's easy for parents to have expectations that don't fit their child at that moment. That's okay—part of parenting is learning compassion, for yourself as much as for your child.

In the challenging moments, when your own sensory systems are telling you to get away from that high-pitched screaming sound as fast as you can, breathe. Say a mantra or rosary. Go take a quick break. Do whatever you need to do to find your sense of calm, to be their beacon in the storm. You know that self-regulation skills are in a part of the brain that continues to develop throughout childhood and even adolescence. You know that there may be a sensory component to the outburst, and that you may be able to tweak something to make life more bearable in the moment.

Remember that each child has their own pattern of growth and development unfolding, and it will be different for every other child (even twins, trust me). By understanding how your child reacts to the sensory information they get and adapting in the moment to give them what they need to feel safe, you are helping them learn about the world. When your child sees you remember those ear protectors, they get a double dose of safety–they know that they won't be overwhelmed during a fun outing, and (arguably more importantly) they know that you have their back.

When your child knows you're in their corner, that you're there to help them through the bad times and celebrate the good ones, it forges a bond between you that's like no other. That relationship you're building with your child will be the very foundation of how they perceive themselves and the world around them, and the cornerstone to their self-soothing skills. The first step to building that foundation is learning how to tune into the cues your child is giving you, so you know how to help.

*Tuning In to Your Kid and Their Cues*

Kids can be really confusing. That's largely because, especially for younger children, they are still learning who they are, what the world is, and what their place is in it. Add in the fact that, depending on their stage of development, they literally can't control their emotions and/or communicate well, it's no wonder they're all over the place! This is where you, the parent or caregiver, can help.

Learning how to really look at your child, at what they do or don't do, say or don't say, and how they go about doing it, is what psychologists refer to as "attunement." Attunement is your ability to be aware and in sync with your child's emotions and signals so you can respond to their needs. If you think about it, we attune with a lot of people, but it takes time. When you first started hanging out with your best friend, you probably didn't realize that when she put on songs by Ani DeFranco it meant she was about to have a fight with her boyfriend. On your first date with your partner, you didn't realize that when they purse their lips that way, it means they're really irritated with you.

It's the same with your kiddo. It takes time to get to know them—and because they're growing and changing so quickly, what you know today probably won't be true forever. This is why the concept of "being a student of my child" is so important. Your ability to observe, notice, remember, and meet your child where they are will not only serve as the building blocks of your relationship, it will help them form a solid foundation for their own sense of self.

In order to do this, tune in to these three things:

- Your child's physical cues
- Your own feelings
- The vibe between you

## Your child's physical cues

This is everything you can observe about their body and facial expressions. It might be an increase in their breathing or heart rate, or them going limp. It could be running away, or hitting, or biting, or screaming. Let yourself really study what's going on with their actual body in the moment, as this will give you information about how their stress response is coming out.

Some things you might look for:

- Rapid or shallow breathing
- Flushed or pale skin
- Dilated pupils
- Sweating
- Fisted hands
- Clenched jaw
- Trembling or shaking
- Upset stomach
- Tapping fingers
- Running or trying to get away
- Avoiding eye contact
- Physically "shrinking" or making self smaller
- Freezing in place
- Headache
- Stomach ache
- Crying
- Screaming
- Rapid speech
- Stuttering
- Inability to speak clearly

## Your own feelings

You are like a barometer for your child in ways you may not be aware of. Remember those mirror neurons go both ways! So, just like tuning in to your child's cues, tune in to your own. You may have some of the physiological cues listed above. You may also (because your brain is more fully developed) be able to identify a variety of emotions coursing through you. Take a moment and label those, if possible. Labeling emotions can take us out of our stress response as it uses a different part of the brain—it's a tool that many parents aren't aware of. Also, having a regular mindfulness practice, even if it's just a few minutes a day, helps to train *your* brain and body on how to focus on the moment and can make this process easier.

## The vibe between you

There is an energy flow that goes back and forth between you and your child. That energy could be labeled as language, or non-verbals, or a dozen other names, but at the end of the day it's the transference of some kind of energy. Pay attention to that. Some parents report feeling "sharp," or, "jagged" energy between them and their child during challenging moments. Or they might say they feel "blocked," "overwhelmed," or "confused." There's no right or wrong way to describe this energy. The important thing is to pay attention and practice tuning in.

## The Tools

Ok, you have a better understanding of how your child's brain and body work together, why they might be losing it, and why you are instrumental in helping them (letting them "borrow your brain.") But what do you do about it?

In this section, you'll find 20 activities to do with your child, during times of joy and connection. **It is critical that you practice these tools during times you and your child are feeling happy to be together.** The trick is to associate these activities with that feeling of connection and closeness.

You'll notice, over time, that your child will start to use some of these tools to help manage their big feelings and overwhelm. But it will take time. Remember this is all about development, and it simply can't be rushed. Each child's development unfolds in a unique way, no matter how much faster we may wish it to happen sometimes! What we can do is set our kids up in a way that supports that growth and development so that conditions are prime. Then when they're ready, there are fewer barriers to actually using these tools and learning the secrets behind self-regulation.

Each activity is labeled with the sensory system(s) activated. Use this information over time to learn what helps calm your child down or ramp your child up. There will be times when they need each, and having this shorthand in your mind will help everyone find the appropriate state of arousal.

Remember these key ingredients for each activity:

- When: connected, calm, regular practice
- Where: safe place
- Who: both of you together
- Why: to associate these activities with you and the sense of peace and love you radiate

Remember that no one will resonate with all of these activities. Try them out to see what works for you and your child both. Also remember that even if it works one time or even ten times, the next time it may not for a multitude of reasons. That's okay! The goal is to spend time regularly with your child with the intention of connecting in the moment.

Finally, a huge part of this is attuning to your child. That means observing your child, yourself, and the vibe between you. There are places for you to write down observations about your child before and after trying each activity, as well as for you to record any reflections you have as you continue to gain insights. Have fun! Each activity is a chance to really enjoy your child.

# *Bell Bowl Meditation*

(auditory)

<u>Materials</u>:
Meditation bowl, bell, or item that rings when struck
Striker

<u>Tuning-in questions before you begin:</u>

- What physiological cues are you noticing in your child?
- What cues are you noticing in yourself?
- What is the vibe between you like?

<u>Activity:</u>
Introduce your child to the bell if this is the first time, or remind them of it if you've used it before.

"This is a special kind of bowl. It doesn't hold food or water or flowers or anything you can touch. Can you guess what it holds? Sound! Let's take a minute to see what sound it makes."

Using the striker, hit the bell gently but hard enough to produce a sound. Let your child have a turn.

"Let's play a little game. Let's hold our pinkies up for as long as we can hear the sound. When you can't hear it anymore, put your pinkie back down. Ready?"

Put pinkies up in the air, close eyes if everyone is comfortable, and strike the bell. Put pinkies back down when you can't hear the sound anymore. Discuss how it might be at different times for each of you and how interesting it is how we're all different.

Based on your child's age, you may only do this for a few minutes. This is perfectly fine. Focus on connection and joy in the moment, and let go of expectations. When your child is done, simply clean up and move on.

<u>Tuning-in questions for afterward</u>:

- What physiological cues are you noticing in your child?
- What cues are you noticing in yourself?
- What is the vibe between you like?

# *Quiet vs Loud*

(auditory)

*Materials*:
Metal bowls or other objects that make noise
Wooden spoons, sticks, etc. to whack those objects

Tuning-in questions before you begin:

- What physiological cues are you noticing in your child?
- What cues are you noticing in yourself?
- What is the vibe between you like?

Activity:
Introduce the main idea. "Let's play Quiet and Loud! First, let's listen to each of these things in front of us." Pick up a wooden spoon and hold it to your ear, then whisper, "Do you think this is quiet or loud?" Do this with a couple more items. Then take a spoon and whack it against one of the objects.

"How about that? Is that quiet or loud? What if we bang these other things together?" Take a little time to explore how different items make different sounds at different volumes.

"What about us? Are we quiet or are we loud?" Discuss a little with your child, pointing out that like the items sometimes we're quiet and sometimes we're loud. "Let's practice being loud!" Yell or sing, banging items together to make noise. NOTE: For kids who are more sensitive to sound, you may need to adjust how loud you get. Tune in to those physiological cues to see how comfortable your child is.

After a few moments, whisper, "Now let's practice being quiet." Place the objects down or hold them close—any ways you can think of to keep things very quiet. Whisper again, "Can we talk and still be quiet? What if we stop talking altogether? What if we're very still and try to be completely silent? Let's try it!" Practice being silent for a few moments.

Alternate between loud and quiet and silent for a few minutes. Keep in mind that young children can generally do a maximum amount of quiet time of one minute per age—it's pretty short. When you see your child is less interested, thank them for playing with you and move on to whatever is next.

Tuning-in questions for afterward:

- What physiological cues are you noticing in your child?
- What cues are you noticing in yourself?
- What is the vibe between you like?

# *Breathing Buddies*

(interoceptive)

<u>Materials</u>:
Small stuffed animals
Comfortable place where you can both lie flat on your back

<u>Tuning-in questions before you begin</u>:

- What physiological cues are you noticing in your child?
- What cues are you noticing in yourself?
- What is the vibe between you like?

<u>Activity</u>:
Introduce the idea. "Let's play a game called 'Breathing Buddies.' We're going to lie on our backs, put our stuffies on our tummies, and then see if we can help our buddy go up and down with our breath." Lie down and demonstrate. "When I breathe in, can you see how they go up? Then when I breathe out, they go back down again. It's like an elevator!"

Encourage your child to lie next to you and slowly breathe in and out, watching the stuffies rise and fall with the breaths. Make sure to have fun with it, and if your child starts to be disinterested let it go and move on to whatever is next. Remember this is a skill you are building, and it may be your child is only willing to play for a minute or two. *Having a good time and connecting while you do this is more important than length of time.*

Tuning-in questions for afterward:

- What physiological cues are you noticing in your child?
- What cues are you noticing in yourself?
- What is the vibe between you like?

# *Snorkel Breathing*

(interoceptive)

<u>Materials</u>:
Straws that bend
Clear, open space you can easily move in

<u>Tuning-in questions before you begin</u>:

- What physiological cues are you noticing in your child?
- What cues are you noticing in yourself?
- What is the vibe between you like?

<u>Activity</u>:
Introduce the idea. "Let's pretend we're swimming in the ocean with a snorkel to help us breathe. Do you know what a snorkel is? It's a special tube that goes from the water up to the surface where there's air. Let's put our snorkels in! Put the smaller end in your mouth, and aim the long part of the straw up where the air is. Now let's practice—we can breathe in through our noses," (pause and breathe in through your nose) "and out through our snorkel" (blow the air out of the straw).

Pretend to swim around the room. Pause from time to time to discuss what creatures you're seeing. Continue to breathe in through the nose, out through the straw. Cue in to your child, and stop when you see they are losing interest.

<u>Tuning-in questions for afterward</u>:

- What physiological cues are you noticing in your child?
- What cues are you noticing in yourself?
- What is the vibe between you like?

# Breath Ball

(interoceptive, proprioceptive)

*Materials*:
Straws
Small pieces of paper (like the wrapping on a straw)
Cups
Clear, open space you can both lie down comfortably in

Tuning-in questions before you begin:

- What physiological cues are you noticing in your child?
- What cues are you noticing in yourself?
- What is the vibe between you like?

Activity:
Introduce the idea. "Let's play some breath ball! First, we lie down on our tummies, facing each other." Lie down, facing each other, a few feet apart. "Now we take this little paper ball, put it in front of us, and blow it back and forth across the floor. Like this!" Blow through your straw to move the paper ball closer to your child.

Once you've both practiced moving the "ball," place the cups down on their sides, near each person. "Now let's see if we can get the ball into the goal!" Practice blowing through the straw to move the paper ball into the cup. Have fun together. If it feels like it's getting too competitive, work as a team, each of you trying to move a ball into a goal while next to each other. Cue in to your child, and stop when you see they're losing interest.

Tuning-in questions for afterward:

- What physiological cues are you noticing in your child?
- What cues are you noticing in yourself?
- What is the vibe between you like?

# *Big, Burly Bubble Breaths*

(interoceptive)

<u>Materials</u>:
1 cup for each of you (with about 1 inch of water and 1 drop of dish soap in it)
Straw for each of you
Table or space where you can spill a little soapy water
Cloths and/or towels to wipe up spills

<u>Tuning-in questions before you begin</u>:

- What physiological cues are you noticing in your child?
- What cues are you noticing in yourself?
- What is the vibe between you like?

<u>Activity</u>:
Introduce the idea. "Wanna make some big, burly bubbles? Let's do it!" Put your straw in your cup, breathe in through your nose, and start blowing out through the straw. Encourage your child to do the same. "Let's see how high we can make the bubbles go!" You can pause from time to time to observe the

bubbles. "Oh, I see rainbows in my bubbles. Aren't they pretty?"

Tune in to your child, and stop when they start to lose interest. This can be a bit messy, so it's important to plan ahead and let that be part of the fun. Use the towels to wipe up any spills and move on.

Tuning-in questions for afterward:

- What physiological cues are you noticing in your child?
- What cues are you noticing in yourself?
- What is the vibe between you like?

# Magic Wands

(interoceptive, visual)

<u>Materials</u>:
Feathers
Popsicle sticks
Tape

<u>Tuning-in questions before you begin</u>:

- What physiological cues are you noticing in your child?
- What cues are you noticing in yourself?
- What is the vibe between you like?

<u>Activity</u>:
Introduce the idea. "Let's make some magic wands! These wands have a special kind of magic. If I'm upset and I make the feathers dance, the magic is I start to feel better. Isn't that cool? First, you choose a feather." Each of you chooses a feather. "Then you tape it to the top of the stick." Demonstrate and help them with tape if needed. "Now watch while I make mine dance." Gently blow out onto the feather and watch it move.

Make as many wands as you like, and be sure to practice making the feather on each one dance. Note: Once your child learns to use this tool more regularly, they are easy to stash in glove compartments, purses, diaper bags, etc. so you can have one on hand if things get rough.

Tuning-in questions for afterward:

- What physiological cues are you noticing in your child?
- What cues are you noticing in yourself?
- What is the vibe between you like?

# *Hot Cocoa Magic*

(olfactory, gustatory)

<u>Materials</u>:
Hot cocoa (or any warm drink with a nice smell)

<u>Tuning-in questions before you begin</u>:

- What physiological cues are you noticing in your child?
- What cues are you noticing in yourself?
- What is the vibe between you like?

<u>Activity</u>:
Introduce the idea. "Let's have a special treat! I made some cocoa for us. Here's yours." Pass them their mug. "Mmm. Can you smell that?" Take a moment to breathe in deeply through your nose, encouraging your child to do the same. "Let's take a small sip." Sip your drink. "Mmmm. I think I'll do that again, but this time I'm going to hold that sip in my mouth a little longer." Do so, closing your eyes and focusing on the tastes in your mouth. "I'm tasting something sweet, and I can really taste the chocolate. What do you taste?" Take turns breathing in the scent and focusing on the

flavors. Try not to have much conversation, but instead focus on experiencing the smell and taste of the drink together. Tune in to your child and move on when they are no longer interested.

<u>Tuning-in questions for afterward</u>:

- What physiological cues are you noticing in your child?
- What cues are you noticing in yourself?
- What is the vibe between you like?

# *Peace In a Jar*

(visual)

<u>Materials</u>:
Clear, sturdy jar with lid
Glitter glue in favorite color(s)
Extra glitter (optional)
Clear dish soap
Kettle or access to hot water (not *too* hot!)
Long spoon or stirrer
Snow globe (or model "Peace In a Jar")

<u>Tuning-in questions before you begin</u>:

- What physiological cues are you noticing in your child?
- What cues are you noticing in yourself?
- What is the vibe between you like?

<u>Activity</u>:
Introduce the idea. Pull out the model globe and show it to your child. "Let's take a look at this globe. Here, you can shake, shake, shake it." Offer to your child so they can shake it. "Now let's set it down and watch it. See how all the little flakes swirl and swirl, and then

gently settle over time? We can think of our thoughts and feelings like that, when they're swirling and swirling. If we sit quietly and breathe, we can feel those thoughts start to settle, just like the flakes in the globe. Let's watch for a moment and see if it works." Sit and watch the flakes settle, minimizing conversation.

"Did you like that? I sure did! Would you like to make one of your own? Great! Let's make one together!"

1. Pour hot water into the jar, filling it about half way. Please take care—if the water is too hot it will make the jar too hot to hold. Check before you let your child touch the jar, adding cold water if necessary.
1. Let your child squeeze the glitter glue into the jar. (The more glue, the slower the globe will settle.)
2. Let your child add in as much extra glitter as they like (optional).
3. Put one drop of dish soap in (too much will make it foamy).
4. Put on lid and shake. See if it settles at a speed your child likes. If it's too slow, add more glue. If it's too fast, add more water.
5. Once you both feel it's just right, put the lid on tightly.

"Now you have your own Peaceful Presence Globe! You can keep that wherever you like. And if you want to, we can make more."

Keep in mind that younger children may get distracted easily and some may not be able to finish the jar on their own. That's okay! Remember the goal is to create time and space to be together. You can also follow up on this activity by getting the jar out at times throughout the week where you both have time to sit and watch the sparkles settle.

Tuning-in questions for afterward:

- What physiological cues are you noticing in your child?
- What cues are you noticing in yourself?
- What is the vibe between you like?

# *Cuddle Meditation*

(interoceptive)

<u>Materials</u>:
Just you and a comfortable, quiet space large enough for you to sit and hold your child

<u>Tuning-in questions before you begin</u>:

- What physiological cues are you noticing in your child?
- What cues are you noticing in yourself?
- What is the vibe between you like?

<u>Activity</u>:
Introduce the idea. "I'm going to sit and do a little meditation. Would you like to join me?" If your child says yes, invite them to sit in your lap.

"Let's have you sit so you can put your ear against my chest. There you go. Now, if we both sit very quietly and still, can you hear my heart beating?" Sit quietly and still, snuggling your child as you do so. After they report being able to hear your heart, you can ask them, "Wonderful. Now listen again, and see if you can hear by breathing, too." Take several long, slow breaths. When they say they can hear you breathing, ask, "Let's see if you can breathe with me. Let's breathe together," and invite them to take long, slow breaths with you.

Continue as long as you're both comfortable, moving on to what's next when you see your child has lost interest.

Tuning-in questions for afterward:

- What physiological cues are you noticing in your child?
- What cues are you noticing in yourself?
- What is the vibe between you like?

# *Feelings Collage*

(visual, tactile)

<u>Materials</u>:
Long sheets of paper
Glue or tape
Markers, crayons, pencils, etc.
Collage materials (scraps of tissue paper, feathers, shells, magazine photos, etc.)
Table or large space to work

<u>Tuning-in questions before you begin</u>:

- What physiological cues are you noticing in your child?
- What cues are you noticing in yourself?
- What is the vibe between you like?

<u>Activity</u>:
Introduce the idea. "Sometimes I like to imagine what my feelings look like. Would you like to make some art with me about feelings?" If your child says yes, invite them to sit in your lap. If they say no or seem resistant, you can say, "That's okay. If you'd like to join me, I'll be here." You can also use this as an opportunity to name

some feelings, "You look a little sad," or, "You sure look happy while you're doing that!"

Lay the paper out. Ask your child if they'd like to make their own or create one with you. As you place different colors or objects down, talk about what feelings you think are associated with them.

Continue as long as you're both comfortable, moving on to what's next when you see your child has lost interest. Once the project has dried (if you use paint or glue), hang it where you'll see it often so you can talk about it. "Remember how we thought the blue colors were sadness?" You can also reference the collage to talk about your own feelings with your child. "I'm feeling a little yellowish-green this morning, which is nervous, along with some of those cotton balls because I want things to feel soft." There are no right or wrong ways to associate feelings with the collage. The goal is to show your child how to identify and express feelings on a more regular basis.

Tuning-in questions for afterward:

- What physiological cues are you noticing in your child?
- What cues are you noticing in yourself?
- What is the vibe between you like?

# *Oooo...or, "Blech?"*

(tactile)

<u>Materials</u>:
Sensory tub, table, bin, or large bowl
Cornstarch
Water
Small items like cars or figures
Tools such as wooden spoons or stirring sticks

<u>Tuning-in questions before you begin</u>:

- What physiological cues are you noticing in your child?
- What cues are you noticing in yourself?
- What is the vibe between you like?

<u>Activity</u>:
Introduce the idea. "Let's make some Ooobleck!" If they say no or seem resistant, you can say, "That's okay. If you'd like to join me I'll be here."

Put some cornstarch into your container. Talk about how soft and dry it feels in your fingers. Slowly add in the water, mixing it together and noticing how it feels different. Scoop some into your hand with your fingers, noticing how it feels hard when you squeeze it, but soft and liquidy when it sits in your palm. Use the small items to play in it, pretending to drive cars through an Oobleck storm, etc.

Keep an eye on your child to see how they react to the sensations. If you sense they're uncomfortable, don't push them to touch it. They can use a tool to interact with it if they like (as can you!), or they can simply watch you. The key is for you to tune in to how they react to this input.

Continue as long as you're both comfortable, moving on to what's next when you see your child has lost interest.

Tuning-in questions for afterward:

- What physiological cues are you noticing in your child?
- What cues are you noticing in yourself?
- What is the vibe between you like?

# *Dinosaur Feet*

(proprioceptive, auditory)

*Materials*:
Just you and a space large enough for you and your child to stomp, jump, and dance in. Also somewhere you can be as loud as you like.

<u>Tuning-in questions before you begin</u>:

- What physiological cues are you noticing in your child?
- What cues are you noticing in yourself?
- What is the vibe between you like?

<u>Activity</u>:
Introduce the idea. "Let's be dinosaurs together! I'm a T-Rex. RAWR!" Begin stomping your feet and roaring, making sure to tune in to your child so you're not overwhelming them.

Explore more kinds of dinosaurs or other creatures that stomp and jump. Explore making big noises like roaring or other animal sounds. Start to associate different feelings with what you're doing. "I'm a T-Rex

and I'm really angry. RAWR!" Or, "I'm a happy, happy
bunny. Hop, hop, hop!" Be sure to tune in to your child
and their cues as you play together.

Continue as long as you're both comfortable, moving
on to what's next when you see your child has lost
interest.

<u>Tuning-in questions for afterward</u>:

- What physiological cues are you noticing in your
  child?
- What cues are you noticing in yourself?
- What is the vibe between you like?

# Cloud Dough

(tactile, proprioceptive, olfactory)

*Materials*:
Flour
Scented baby oil
Sensory tub, bin, table, or large bowl
Measuring cups/spoons
Wooden spoons, stirring ticks, whisk
Small bowls, ice cube trays, sand molds, small shovels, and other sand toys

Tuning-in questions before you begin:

- What physiological cues are you noticing in your child?
- What cues are you noticing in yourself?
- What is the vibe between you like?

Activity:
Introduce the idea. "Let's make some cloud dough! Can you help me measure?" If they say no or seem resistant, you can say, "That's okay. If you'd like to join me, I'll be here."

Measure out 8 parts flour to 1 part oil. (If you're making a large batch, that would be 8 cups of flour and 1 cup of oil.) Pour the flour first, then slowly mix in the oil using your hands or stirring tools. You'll know it's mixed in when the dough holds its shape in your hand like wet sand.

Play together with your child, exploring the different items and how they work in the dough. Talk about how it feels and smells, and tune in to how they're reacting. If you notice they don't like to touch the dough, encourage them to explore with some of the tools available. You might also offer to let them wear gloves, but keep in mind the goal is to explore together while enjoying the time. This isn't the time to push if they're not having fun.

Continue as long as you're both comfortable, moving on to what's next when you see your child has lost interest.

Tuning-in questions for afterward:

- What physiological cues are you noticing in your child?
- What cues are you noticing in yourself?
- What is the vibe between you like?

## *Silent Helpers*

(auditory, tactile)

<u>Materials</u>:
Large beads with different textures and colors
Beading string or twine
Break-away clasp (for necklaces)
Scissors
Small mat or cloth for each of you

<u>Tuning-in questions before you begin</u>:

- What physiological cues are you noticing in your child?
- What cues are you noticing in yourself?
- What is the vibe between you like?

<u>Activity</u>:
Introduce the idea. "Let's make some silent helpers. These are special bracelets or necklaces that help us be very, very quiet and listen." If they say no or seem resistant, you can say, "That's okay. If you'd like to join me, I'll be here."

Place a mat in front of each of you, and then select a few beads to place on it. Take a moment to "listen" to each bead, and talk about how it feels. "I'm going to listen to my beads with my fingers. Let's see, this one feels very soft and smooth. This one is all bumpy and funny! This one feels pointy," and so on. Lay the beads on the mat in the order you want to string them. Ask your child how long they want their string to be and cut it for them or, if you're comfortable, have them do that for both of you. Once the beads are laced, tie the ends together so they form a loop. Then practice "listening" to your silent helpers, whispering about how each bead feels.

Continue as long as you're both comfortable, moving on to what's next when you see your child has lost interest.

Tuning-in questions for afterward:

- What physiological cues are you noticing in your child?
- What cues are you noticing in yourself?
- What is the vibe between you like?

# *Rainbow Bubble Painting*

(visual, interoceptive)

*Materials*:
Large area that can get a little messy
Bubble solution and wands
Food coloring
Small bowls (one for each food color)
Large sheet of white paper
Masking tape
Drop cloth (if indoors)
Music (optional)

Tuning-in questions before you begin:

- What physiological cues are you noticing in your child?
- What cues are you noticing in yourself?
- What is the vibe between you like?

Activity:
Introduce the idea. "Let's paint with some bubbles! First we'll make some different colors of bubble juice." Lay the drop cloth down, then put out the bowls. Pour enough bubble solution into each bowl to easily dip a

bubble wand into. Add a few drops of color to each bowl, stirring with the bubble wand, until you get the color you want. You may want to add more color or solution once you start blowing bubbles—let yourself experiment.

Once you have the colored bubble solution, tape the paper to a wall or other vertical surface. You can create one painting together, or if your child prefers, you can each make your own. Model breathing in through your nose and then out slowly through your mouth to make the bubble, blowing very close to the paper. You'll see the bubbles burst on the paper, leaving the color behind. Play some quiet music if you like while you both explore how close to get, how hard to blow, how much color you like, etc.

Continue as long as you're both comfortable, moving on to what's next when you see your child has lost interest.

Tuning-in questions for afterward:

- What physiological cues are you noticing in your child?
- What cues are you noticing in yourself?
- What is the vibe between you like?

# Special Stones

(tactile, interoceptive)

*Materials*:
8" cloth circles with pre-cut holes around edges (can be done with hole puncher), one for each of you
Smocks
Fabric markers
Ribbons in 16" lengths
Scissors
Tapestry needles
Several large, smooth pebbles

Tuning-in questions before you begin:

- What physiological cues are you noticing in your child?
- What cues are you noticing in yourself?
- What is the vibe between you like?

Activity:
Introduce the idea. "Let's find your special stone today, and then make a little bag to hold it."

Spread the stones in front of both of you, and help your child connect to each one. You might say something like this: "Choose a stone, close your eyes, and hold it in your hand. Notice how it feels in your hand—if it's rough or smooth, heavy or light. Breathe in through your nose and listen to the deep quiet inside. Feel how the quiet inside that stone connects to your belly, how you have the same quiet inside. Breathe in again, bringing the quiet of the stone into your belly. When you feel that deep quiet inside of you, open your eyes." Invite them to choose another stone or two, until they have one they feel is "the quietest."

Next, use the markers to decorate the cloth. While the markers dry, thread the needle with the ribbon. Weave the needle in and out of the holes in the cloth until it cinches up into a bag. Place the special pebble inside, letting your child know if they find more special stones they can also live in this bag.

Tuning-in questions for afterward:

- What physiological cues are you noticing in your child?
- What cues are you noticing in yourself?
- What is the vibe between you like?

# *Thankful Hands*

(tactile)

<u>Materials</u>:
Quiet space for you and your child to sit comfortably.
Paper and pencil

<u>Tuning-in questions before you begin</u>:

- What physiological cues are you noticing in your child?
- What cues are you noticing in yourself?
- What is the vibe between you like?

<u>Activity</u>:
Introduce the idea. "Today we're going to find 5 things we're thankful for and do a special meditation using our hands. What are some things you're thankful for?" Write down each one. If your child has trouble thinking of some, write down some things you're thankful for until you have at least five.

Hold out one hand, and with the index finger of the other hand point to the base of your thumb. Say the first thing you're thankful for ("I'm thankful for _____"), then breathe in while you trace your thumb up to the top, and breathe out while you trace your thumb back down and to the base of the finger next to it. Say the next thing on your thankful list, breathe in while you trace that finger to the top, and breathe out while you trace it back down and to the base of the finger next to it. Repeat this for all five fingers. When you reach the end, put both hands together, breathe in and out again, and say, "I am thankful."

This activity can easily turn into a regular practice. It can be done before meals, right before bed, etc. Be sure to tune in to your child each time, and if they're not ready in the moment, you can model it for them, saying your own thankfuls.

Tuning-in questions for afterward:

- What physiological cues are you noticing in your child?
- What cues are you noticing in yourself?
- What is the vibe between you like?

# *Swing & Sing*

(vestibular)

<u>Materials</u>:
Space large enough for you and another adult to swing your child comfortably
Blanket or cloth large enough to hold your child, but small enough you and another adult can pick the child up inside of it while holding onto the corners

<u>Tuning-in questions before you begin:</u>

- What physiological cues are you noticing in your child?
- What cues are you noticing in yourself?
- What is the vibe between you like?

<u>Activity:</u>
Introduce the idea. "Let's swing you in your blanket!"

Lay the blanket/cloth on the floor flat and have your child lay on top of it, on their back. You and the other adult stand at the head and feet of your child, then reach down and pick up the two corners. Gently and carefully, stretch the blanket out until you're holding your child above the floor, like a hammock. Gently swing them back and forth while singing a soft song together.

Continue as long as you're both comfortable, moving on to what's next when you see your child has lost interest.

<u>Tuning-in questions for afterward</u>:

- What physiological cues are you noticing in your child?
- What cues are you noticing in yourself?
- What is the vibe between you like?

# Spin & Grin

(vestibular)

<u>Materials</u>:
Large outdoor space on a soft area, like grass or rubberized playground

<u>Tuning-in questions before you begin</u>:

- What physiological cues are you noticing in your child?
- What cues are you noticing in yourself?
- What is the vibe between you like?

<u>Activity</u>:
Introduce the idea. "Let's do some spinning!" If your child looks uncomfortable or says no, respect that in the moment and try this activity another time.

Hold your child's hands firmly in yours, and start to spin in a circle. Spin just fast enough for their feet to come slightly off the ground. After a couple of spins, set them down as you both collapse onto your backs. Talk about how that felt for each of you, if things are still spinning, if it felt fun, etc.

Continue as long as you're both comfortable, moving on to what's next when you see your child has lost interest.

<u>Tuning-in questions for afterward</u>:

- What physiological cues are you noticing in your child?
- What cues are you noticing in yourself?
- What is the vibe between you like?

## Conclusion

Remember the most important factor in all of these activities is the relationship between you and your child. While there are times to push something, for yourself and for them, these activities are not designed with that goal in mind. Choose the ones that feel easy for you both, find a time and space that feel relaxing and secure. Involve any parenting partners or other caregivers from time to time (you'll need one for the *Swing & Sing*). Tune in to your child, yourself, and the energy between you.

As you continue on through this amazing journey of parenthood, be as kind to yourself as you are to your child. You'll notice over time that your child will take in those lessons and choose kindness when interacting with others. You'll see their self-regulation skills blossom and bloom. And you'll realize that the little voice inside your head that used to scold you every time is more gentle and forgiving.

If you enjoyed this book, you may also like:

You can find this and other books by Kristene Geering
in your Amazon marketplace.

Want to learn more?
www.letuslearntogether.com

Made in the USA
Middletown, DE
11 September 2024

60215594R00040